Go and play

Story written by Cynthia Rider
Illustrated by Tim Archbold

Speed Sounds

Consonants   *Ask children to say the sounds.*

f	l	m	n	r	s	v	z	sh	**th**	ng
ff	ll		nn		ss	**ve**	zz			**nk**
							s			

b	c	d	g	h	j	p	qu	t	w	x	y	**ch**
bb	k		gg					tt	wh			tch
	ck											

Each box contains one sound but sometimes more than one grapheme.
*Focus graphemes for this story are **circled**.*

Vowels

Ask children to say the sounds in and out of order.

a	e	i	o	u
at	hen	in	on	up

ay	ee	igh	ow	oo
day	see	high	blow	zoo

Story Green Words

Max   Mum   Jack   Dad   sun   hat   lost

much   wet   just   back

Ask children to read the root first and then the whole word with the suffix.

fit → fits

Red Words

Ask children to practise reading the words across the rows, down the columns and in and out of order clearly and quickly.

said	to	the
go	I	she
now	play*	my
too*	no	you

* Red Word in this book only

Go and play

Introduction

Do you like watching TV? Max does, even when it's a nice sunny day. His mum wants him to go outside and play. She tells him to turn the TV off and find a sun hat. Max says he's lost it, but he doesn't want to wear anyone else's sun hat instead!

"Put that TV off," said Mum.

"Put on a sun hat and go and play."

"I have lost my sun hat,"
said Max.

"Put on Dad's sun hat then," said Mum.

"Much too big!"
said Max.

"Put on my sun hat then," said Mum.

"Much too pink!"
said Max.

Mum got Jack's sun hat.

"This fits," she said.
"Now, go and play!"

"Much too wet!"
said Max.

"I will just have to put the TV back on!"

Questions to talk about

Ask children to TTYP for each question using 'Fastest finger' (FF) or 'Have a think' (HaT).

pp.8–9 (HaT)   Why does Max think he can't go out and play?

p.10 (FF)   Whose hat is much too big for Max?

p.11 (FF)   Whose hat does Max think is too pink?

p.12 (FF)   Whose hat fits?

p.13 (FF)   Why can't Max go out and play?

      (HaT)   Do you think he's disappointed?